WITHE

A SENSE OF PLACE

A PLACE OF SENSE

LIMERICKS FOR

THE LIGHTHOUSE

by : GODFREY HOLMES

Godfrey H. Holmes

July 2019

© Godfrey Holmes

April 2019

ISBN : 978-0-9934644-4-7

NETHERMOOR BOOKS

"St. Elphin,"

12 North Promenade

Withernsea

HU19 2DP

Telephone : 01964-615258

Contact the Author:
godfrey.holmes@btinternet.com

The full price of any Copy sold will be donated to the Withernsea Lighthouse Trust. However, all viewpoints or standpoints expressed in this Verse are entirely those of the Author – independent of the Trust; independent of supporters of the Trust.

Dedicated

to

Carolyn & Paul

****

High above the wild Ocean
A Tower stands;
High above the bustling Promenade
A Tower stands;
High above make-and-take far below
A Tower stands;
And in the distance -
'Neath the sun & moon & stars -
A Tower stands.

****

THE LIMERICK

IS A POETIC FORM:
POPULARIZED BY THE POET, ARTIST,
HUMOURIST & MUSICIAN

EDWARD LEAR [1812-88]...

A STRUCTURE OFTEN ASSUMED TO BE HUMOUROUS
OR BAWDY - OR BOTH.

BUT LIMERICKS CAN ALSO BE VERY <u>SERIOUS</u> -

& CAN CERTAINLY SHOW WIT & WISDOM
WITHOUT RESORT TO INDECENCY OR SPITE.

THE EXACT FORMAT OF A LIMERICK IS :

***** FIVE LINES - 1,2,3,4,5... & FIVE LINES ONLY.

***** LINE <u>TWO</u> SHOULD RHYME OR HALF-RHYME
WITH LINE NUMBER <u>ONE</u> -

***** ALSO WITH LINE NUMBER <u>FIVE</u>.

***** EQUALLY, LINES <u>THREE</u> & <u>FOUR</u>
SHOULD RHYME....

***** LINES THREE & FOUR ARE FREQUENTLY <u>SHORTER</u>
THAN ALL OTHER LINES.

***** OF INTEREST, THERE IS NO REQUIREMENT WHATEVER
FOR A LIMERICK TO START WITH THE WORDS :
"THERE ONCE WAS A..."

****

WITHERNSEA :
A SENSE OF PLACE
A PLACE OF SENSE
Limericks for the Lighthouse

A Place with the freshest air ;
An int'resting Place to share !
Where everyone reaches
Nine, ten, sun-kissed Beaches -
Read on ! But of Satire beware !

Wiv once was a new-found-land:
Defined by sea & fine sand...
A Place to remember
From March to December...
Brighton outclassed - & *more grand ?*

Pilgrims they surely were :
Explorers - if you prefer.
With true Viking verve
They held their nerve :
Nothing would Cave-men deter.

Clay underfoot was quite heavy -
And Parli'ment wanted a Levy.
Some farmsteads were scattered:
Grown grain all that mattered -
When Tourists arrived, in a bevy !

Junes, then, were extremely pleasant
For even the chilliest Peasant
Who *liked* his first Summer ;
[Past-August much glummer !]
Bread spread with paté of pheasant ?

Too soon those four months of *cool:*
Ice-patterns that cause folk to drool ;
Harsh test of survival :
So soon post-arrival ;
Abroad only servant or fool.

The Esplanade had to come first
[And how grumpy Settlers cursed !]
When new money arrived
They felt more deprived :
Their lot, Fate decreed, the worst.

Withernsea *did* get a Railway link:
Bannister's dream laid down in a blink !
Broderick's fine Station
For day-trip - vacation ? -
Fares Cheaper than most would think.

How Wiv's *first* Pier was badly battered
[Ships through its timbers clattered]
Full length shrank in stages
[How storm's anger rages!]
Founding dreams so rudely shattered !

In sunshine, *Pier Towers* are golden :
To Conway their builders beholden.
In all there are four -
Seen right down the Shore :
Enough a *new* Pier to embolden ?

Long Promenades also were raised :
Their promoters quite unfazed.
They even piped Gas,
Telephones, alas!
[Their ingenuity praised]

A stranger must understand
A Lighthouse built far inland !
Standing so tall:
So solid each wall !
Tickets bought on demand.

Magnificent views from the top;
Tourists urged not to flop
After all that clamber -
Kay Kendall's dress amber -
Withernsea's clustered backdrop.

" Mum : are we half way there ?
I can't do another Stair!
We've been round and round:
So far from the ground !
My shoes are beginning to wear...."

And during past Golden Age
Prized Minstrels did not renege
On their promise to act -
Tossed coins to exact? -
So buoyed on Withernsea's stage !

Showboats swung on the Sands,
Stunts, stilts and contests grand !
All sorts of fun,
Cheap toys to be won !
Outings not ending as planned ?

Bank Holiday Beaches were packed:
Nearness fun-seekers scarce lacked!
They came in their scores:
To *wider* Outdoors !
[This Resort had everything cracked !]

Pre-fridge, warmth got to the ices;
For the seller: melting, a crisis.
" Far safer buy rock
Or a new Summer frock ! "
With children in tow : sacrifices.

Youngsters wore quite formal suits -
Breaches & bonnets cute -
" Like little grown men " :
[No halfway stage then !]
Prim grown-ups upholding repute.

9

Then there were bathers *nude*
Which wasn't considered rude !
They tasted the waters
Away from their daughters!
[*So rarely afeared of the Prude*]

Did they *really* take Switchback ride ?
Did they free-skate side-to-side ?
What made up their fun
'Neath watery Sun ?
[Head home - or sodden abide ?]

Did they *really* lift up the oar:
Five-foot above blue Lake's new floor ?
How hard did they paddle
In wood boats to straddle ?
[How oft was shore's summons ignored !]

Did they *really* see Village Model?
[Next Mere - where Mallards did waddle ?]
Each construct so slender !
With mini fire-tender !
Each bairn, each pet, mollycoddle ?

Did they *really* attend Hollym Races :
Eventing which left so few traces ?
Remarkable cheering
When finish-line nearing !
[Punters astride their suitcases!]

Did they *really* play serious Tennis ?
"Set One, 40-love, to Dennis !"
Who owned cat-gut Racquet ?
In Middle-Class bracket ?
Florins to hand - not pennies.

Did they *really* play crown-green bowls ?
On turf needing soft crèpe soles?
" Where's heading the Jack ? "
" Whose throw shows the knack ? "
[A Game not relying on Goals !]

And did they *really* use Pool external?
[Brisk exercise: natural, eternal   ]
Practising strokes
[No booze & no smokes !]
Just outclass each slowcoach infernal !

Did they *really*   get thrown out of lodgings ?
[Fierce Landladies' rampage wise dodging ?]
So few coins for spending -
More borrowed : *not lending.*
[Much make-do & no little codging ?]

A few day trippers had bikes
[A few more had invalid trikes]
Those days of bone-shaking
[What risks riders taking !]
Or strolling, more to their likes ?

Wiv was built by jobbing Spec-Builder :
Short leases so writ to bewilder !
Or Sale to one's Neighbour
To pay for more labour
[A Home fit for Alf & Matilda ?]

And those Porches ceramically tiled !
[Function & Art reconciled]
A prized North-facing Larder !
[Stone floors seem much harder !]
Pan-Closet: "out-in-the-wild" !

Population speed'ly doubled :
All that brickwork ; all that rubble !
House rows built on spec :
Mixed standards ? No check ?
[*Hired joiners joining the Bubble*]

Some housing provided *good* rooming
For people with nemesis looming ?
Caught by recession ?
[The Great Depression ?]
Some quick bucks, or odd jobs, presuming ?

One Street is named after *Cammidge.*
[Mercifully free of much damage !]
He's one of Wiv's founders
[Not one of life's Bounders]
Some gain wealth through prudent marriage !

One Street is named after Cheverton.
[P'raps a supporter of Everton ?]
He loved the Seaside :
South Prom trim - and wide -
Best seen when all bad weather's gone !

Another road honours James Young
[Distinguished Townsmen among]
It led to Band-Stage
[Wiv's pre-Streaming age !]
Thereon could his praises be sung.

The Street that is named for *a Queen*
Camilla Shand's already seen !
Queen Vic never rode it...
Nor Queen Mary strode it...
Our Queen should really have been !

On one Street that's named after *Walter :*
Where Witnesses have their High Altar ;
And Fire Station best sited
For arsonists blighted ?
Bus drivers nip down, neither falter.

Intently, prestige was sought :
Better folk coastward brought ?
But Southport's ambition
Matched Bournemouth's position.
[Brid's wild card: its Fishing Port]

14

Meanwhile this Town has *a grid* :
Straight streets with few buildings hid.
Parallel roads -
Each with Post-Codes.
[Who visits for *en suite* must bid !]

Lost mem-ries: gentle tea-dances ;
Foxtrot, Quickstep... Romances !
Sax-ophonist downbeat ;
Trumpeters *up* beat ;
Pianists aware of side-glances ?

'Neath Parasols Ladies would walk -
Hushed tones their earnest talk :
These *not* servant lasses -
But aspirant Classes
[No squalid conquests to chalk !]

Beer: only a couple of pence :
Warm surrounds; atmosphere dense.
Cradling dwindling cup
Till hearing: "Drink Up !"
[*Another* Inn the where & the whence]

Some Youths would sleep under tents :
Exhausted savings' extent ?
They ate humble pie :
On coarse mats to lie -
Till back t'wards Bradford they went !

When nobody handled much money :
Deprivation didn't sound funny.
With ends forced to meet -
Despair's cry discreet ?
[Line slung to catch the odd tunny]

Penny or tupp'ny machines
Gobbled many-a fun-seekers' means.
Who gained the windfall
[Glance-favoured pin-ball ?]
At Sunset saw winnings so lean.

Entertainment rather dull ?
So toffs jigged the more in Hull.
Withernsea down in the dumps ?
[Wessies not short of grumps !]
Empty pockets - but beaches full !

Five Chippies were owned by *Redfern's :*
The gaffer was Len - with sideburns.
They sold, too, wet plaice,
Fried chicken - with taste :
Whilst staff at the range took their turns.

Jackson's: the Grocer old-fashioned
Served shoppers quite quiet - or passioned.
Their Store at the Junction
Displayed no compunction
Selling Bacon so recently rationed.

Frost's sold so much fresh fruit ;
Spuds, parsnips, beans, beetroot.
Eggs by the Dozen
[A treat for your Cousin !]
And Partridges shot in the shoot.

Where once folk enjoyed late-night clubbing:
Prized promont'ry site took a drubbing :
Sun Terrace with boarding
[No Pirates marauding !]
Now young'uns go more for Hull-Pubbing.

On the Beach they have high wind-shields
For North Wind which sharp cutlass wields.
" Put on that tweed jacket ! "
" Flat cap: did you pack it ? "
" To think: once our raincoats we peeled ! "

And on each Bonfire Night
The skies are with rockets alight.
Just look at the blaze !
[Midst No-vember's haze !]
" Finale" is still the best sight !

And *when* Christmas Lights are switched on :
The Old Year so ruefully gone ?
Just hear the loud cheers
When Santa appears !
Street-sellers by Lamp-posts outshone.

And *if* you've promptly inquired -
And *if* you're prop'ly attired :
From Social Club [Boating]
You'll come out gloating...
[Members : *No Boat required !*]

Glasshouses look rather bare:
Few plants or shrubs flourish there.
No Alpines, no heather,
No Chrysanths to weather ?
Green skills less ready to share ?

The *fields* are adorned with ripe Rape :
Bright yellow making folks gape !
Of all English flowering,
This most o'erpowering...
No need in the future to vape !

Summer brings Elvis pretenders:
Silk-suited - with woven suspenders.
Cliff, Bruce, Stevie, Cilla :
Scores true to scintilla !
[Each Tribute great following renders]

" Yes: it's ' Presley ' I'm wanting to meet :
In Valley Gardens to greet.
He knows every word ;
Wears costume absurd ?
To Gracelands he now retreats ! "

Which tribute compels you to stand :
On Stage, in front of the Band ?
Is it Barry ? Is it Roy ?
[Rolling Stone : greater joy ?]
Some music : live, some canned.

We also have young baton-holders :
Earning their high-mark grade folders.
They twist & they twirl,
Clutched flags to unfurl :
Shy girls : each Performance much bolder.

Girl *dancers* have dance-practice weekly :
" *Move swifter ! *" "* Inherit space meekly ! *"
Hip-hop - or tango ;
Red costumes - or mango.
[Ballet *out of doors* tackled sleekly]

Verity-Lee runs *her own* School of Dancing :
Imperfect routines never chancing.
She asks girls for sequence :
Deft moves born of frequence.
[Guys: don't think they're only prancing !]

And what of the pedal-bike ?
[In Towns most cyclists like]
Why not join a Club ?
[Yorkshire's quite a bike hub !]
Mid-road still better than dyke !

When Withernsea's part of *Le Tour*
Top Cyclists may pass your front door :
The fastest in yellow:
Superior fellow !
[Some backsides by saddle made sore]

And when youth take to the saddle
Challenge will not their wits addle !
They'll need some persistence -
Mounts without assistance ? -
" Who'll rate pedal over *paddle* ? "

Withernsea also has *horses*
Whose speed no one enforces :
Let loose on the sand,
Their gallop so grand...
Which gives us horses for courses !

Each day observe a brown Spaniel:
His Biblical name is *Daniel.*
He gives folk great joy :
Slather ! Annoy !
And siring this Pup is *Nathaniel.*

Some homes keep hounds and Alsatians...
Pugs, bull-dogs - or spotted Dalmatians ?
See poodles cross-bred,
And collies well-fed...
Jack Russells : one priest's appellation.

Of *cats* our streets have but few :
Seen sometimes: a kitten new !
They're generally wary :
Of dogs they feel scary !
Give each Ginger Tom his due.

Most homes keep the sea-gulls at bay :
Those vultures with heads white and grey...
Who flee for their lives,
Then feed their good wives :
Not really bad birds of prey ?

22

Do not make our sea-gulls too tame
[These scavengers get a bad name !]
They'll swoop on your cornet,
Buzz past like a hornet.
[Nicked sandwich no cause for shame !]

Withernsea has but a dozen cows :
Whatever farm finance allows.
Instead we have wheat -
And some sugar-beet...
So milk-stools give way to the plough.

And where are those fields full of sheep ?
Where do those little lambs peep ?
Our Shepherds are few -
Saved for barley crops new -
Farm Subsidies in pockets deep ?

At *Northfield :* an Organ Society !
[Piped music of hugest variety !]
Jazz, Film, Op'ra, Symphony
On Keyboard - with Timpani !
Tunes *spiritual* nurture their Piety.

Wiv *does* have an Army platoon :
For camouflaged youngsters, a boon !
Cadets find a hobby
[All clear of the Bobby !]
Conscription will come all too soon ?

Footy's *part* of each Sunday's ritual :
Played best before plated victuals !
Dads & Lads do the shouting.
Visiting Teams like the outing ?
[Blaming the Ref : habitual !]

Your team: it appears on your shirt ;
If SPURS: that is bound to hurt.
Why not back MAN.CITY ?
[You'll never face pity !]
Or with SCUNTHORPE you might flirt.

Our Golf Course is par Seventy-Two:
Best done when your worst shots are few !
You'll go out in forty;
Less back - if you're naughty !
Each Member knows you through and
through.

When thirsty, folk *first use "The Pier "*;
Then try *"The Commercial "* [austere ?]....
Move on to "The Station" -
Then feel much elation :
"The Plough " serves a perfect guest beer.

Pass by our "new" *Lifeboat Station:*
Affirming unpaid dedication !
Light, fast, rubber dinghy
[Some donors so mingy !]
Those rescued : filled with elation ?

Our Town boasts a new *Policing* Station:
Cause of great Expectation.
They'll catch all those Thieves !
And grant no Reprieves !
What gives rogues their motivation ?

Don't miss Wiv's War-Mem-orials :
Hushed sites of silence Mayorial.
[Remembering each Hero
Whose future proved Zero
In Trenches whose stench was corporeal]

On Proms you turn Left or Right:
1-80 degrees in your sight.
Instead of three-sixty
[With Valleys betwixt ye]
Go boldly into the Night !

On South Prom: a big private boatyard
For Skippers who know they must sail hard.
They mend, scour & varnish
Each rail that might tarnish ;
Upturned, there's a hull to be tarred !

The fountains: they're playing up high ;
They might even reach your thigh !
They've got them in Hull !
So life's never dull.
Let's hope they their critics defy.

The *end* of South Promenade:
Appears on an old Postcard.
It hasn't changed much :
Since founding plans such.
[*Though newer homes sometimes jarred*]

Spot magnificent Billboards [twenty ?]
Engage passers-by aplenty.
In stark black-&-white:
An historian's *delight !*
Nostalgia, regret, as blent be.

" Is it safe to stand in the Ocean? "
" Yes - if you apply Sun Lotion."
" Your spotted bikini
Is daringly weeny ! "
" Sand games : for ills the best potion ! "

Folk love to go step-counting each :
Descending with bliss to the beach.
Or *up* one-by-one
To catch setting Sun.
" On stairs you might Heaven reach ! "

" Can you pass my bucket & spade ? "
" Do I crawl on my tummy - or wade ? "
"On each hottest day
On the beach I will play "
[Of such fun are pastimes made]

Some days we're afraid of high waves :
Great fun - or a watery grave ?
Davy-Jones' locker :
Still comes as shocker
To they whom no life-belt can save.

The nearness of drowning's so real
Yet Tempest's excitement we feel!
Mortality's waiting -
The storm now abating -
Neptune's cull - with no appeal.

When waves aren't so fierce and so high -
No spray rising right up to the sky ! -
Seals swim quite near :
Their playful pups dear !,
Heading back South, by and by.

On still Sea, folk lie out flat
[Each like a wind-blown hat ?]
" *What joy now to float :*
I could be a boat ! "
....If not in " Old Boatshed " sat !

The lads swim in Lycra trunks :
Lasses all loving these hunks !
Or plain pants they wear -
When sent in for a dare
[Like biscuits all out for the dunk]

Forbidden to ride a Skateboard
[Upsetting frail neighb'ly accord ?]
Rollerblades too -
Even Segways *few*....
Forbidden to break from the hordes ?

Kayaks have replaced Canoes :
For paddling, if you so choose.
It's very exciting:
Beating sand kiting...
" If sea-sick, just keep off the booze ! "

We're left with a single Mere :
Deeper than first appears.
It's open for fishing...
For passers-by wishing
They'd paid for some snork'lling gear.

One Angler competes for his prize:
On hook, line & rod Rod relies.
A two-kilo cod !
[Thanksgiving to God !]
Best bait was a dangled surprise !

Offshore are a great deal of Crab
[Washed, dressed: their taste is ab fab !]
They're caught in wood cages
[Full growth may take ages   ]
" And now you must fillet your Dab ! "

Wind *turbines* stand out in the deep :
Energy costs downwards to keep....
Their huge blades go round :
Not making a sound ?
" Climb ladder - and have a peep ! "

Day-break on a Winter morning :
Runners running - but, weary, yawning.
Daily Mails on Sale :
Good read - without fail ?
Is front page uplift - or a warning ?

Our Prom draws a blanket of fog
[" No sight of you on your jog ! "]
So take a strong lamp
To shine on the ramp....
" And borrow your neighbour's Guide Dog ! "

Is that Flamborough that we see?
[Fine headland, you'll agree !]
Flamborough's beams add to four;
Take four breaths, four more....
Night-time's infinity !

" In Withernsea's harshest December :
' Tis East Wind you'll most remember !
Each Northerly blast
Will leave you aghast...
Till following 1st. of September ! "

" You're buying a Dormobile ?
Your bed behind steering-wheel ! "
Sleeping at kerbside:
From locals best hide !
Your breakfast no seagull must steal ! "

For fifty weeks of the year
Hell's Angels come not here.
They travel elsewhere
In search of fresh air -
Lest Vespas should re-appear !

Each trundling mobility scooter
Is fitted with unused hooter.
Will *you* be flattened ?
[A.& E. fattened?]
Who's needing a Penalty Shooter ?

" Beware broken glass in the street ;
Or hid in sand 'neath young feet ?
Glass gives us clear sight -
And drinks, to delight....
Yet misplaced : its harm is complete."

Wiv still has six curio dealers :
Twixt Chemist Shops staffed by healers.
Gems, antiques & junk -
Loot not to debunk !
[Oak pews, stained glass, & kneelers]

"Give to *Gateway !* "- some folk are told -
"And bring in whate'er can be sold ! "
Don't trust the Car Boot
But in attics root
For tools or Silver or Gold.

Posh clothing makes *Dove House* good cash:
Clothing pre-loved - or rash !
Plus discarded Games
With forsaken names !
Dove House has no house-room for trash.

The *LIONS* will sell you electrics-
And Carpet Squares pre-metric !
They do draw keen browsers
[In Shorts - or flared trousers!]
New babies require the obstetric !

Heron's our Grocer local :
Its staunchest custom quite vocal ;
Its prices most reasonable
[Defection quite treasonable !]
Compare each pack ; ask each Yokel.

" At Poundstretch, we'll buy for our Party :
Each plateful will look very arty !
In a field near to Tesco
We'll eat all-alfresco...
The parson, replete, hale and hearty ! "

ALDI's reach has remarkably grown :
Low prices not hitherto known !
The items folk favour
Are sweet - with no flavour :
From distant aerodromes flown !

ALDI has a middle Aisle :
Assorted goods in a pile.
They're not this time edible :
Some bargains incredible.
Our shopping might take quite a while !

Tesco was quite a late-comer
To brighten each shopper's Summer.
Built on a Siding
It soon took a hiding
From Proudfoot's owner glummer.

You might *want a few Souvenirs:*
How your day at the Seaside appears ?
A pretty tea-towel ?
Glazed gull - or lace owl ?
Fridge-magnets & cups full of cheer.

" Where can we buy some ice-cream ? "
" Without it, our babe will scream ! "
" Best try local makes ! "
" Whipped cornets - with Flakes ? "
[Some flavours truly off-beam]

Wiv's Post Office serves lots of senders ;
Notes dished out to folk on their benders.
Some parcels returning
To warehouses churning
More packets for agents & lenders.

Wiv *used to* have three good Banks
Where folks' spare cash - not much ! - sank.
Trippers *do* like real money
[Direct Debit seems funny ?]
And the chimney pot's rather dank !

One Caff has its pre-Season clients -
On Bac'n-&-Eggs quite reliant.
They all love the chatter
Till 5 - when they scatter!
[Their sausages lean, fat - or giant !]

Munching that fresh currant scone
[A little more soft than your phone !]
Press each of its buttons
[Gulp down like a glutton ?]
And now it's your dog's favoured bone !

Of "Instant" be duly tight-lipped:
Just like brown hot water when sipped ?
But with *strong* roast coffee
Buy cake made of toffee,
And ask for your milk to be whipped.

Queen Street *has good places to eat*
If you don't want to eat on a seat.
" Pavlova rice ? "
" Plum crumble is nice ! "
"...And do have some veg. with your meat."

Past Midnight a Pizza queue :
Sent also to fetch some lamb stew.
On a plateful of spuds :
"Those kebabs look duds ! "
"And when are the Noodles due ? "

Does our Town value home cooking ?
For saucepans are residents looking ?
Or do they prefer
This chore to defer ....
And ring to secure Table Booking ?

Markets belong to the past ?
[Rather too makeshift to last ?]
We do have one stall :
Outside, near the wall.
Their flowers sell really fast !

On high street, pass two high street bookies :
Attracting some high-rolling rookies.
Whatever the horse -
[Fifth back o'er the Course ?]
Yields stale crust instead of rich cookies !

You can then bet on League Cup Winners :
On Forwards : in Sin-bins the Sinners ?
Who'll get a Nil Draw ?
Score two goals - or four ?
[Life's rarely a stream of free Dinners]

Bingo promises, too, greater riches
[The Caller will have you in stitches !]
" Sweet Seventy-Seven:
Get ready for Heaven ! "
Your Card - very tempting - bewitches.

In Arcades folk spend their shillings :
To lose all these Punters seem willing !
Slots hungry they choose,
Four fruits to peruse :
New gamblers with coin tubs round milling.

Coin-sweeps are by far most deceptive -
Of ten-pees inviting, receptive.
The next heap will fall
Once you've given your all :
Fools' judgment most keenly perceptive ?

" And never need you spend one pound :
Just keep walking round and around !
Watch the grieving of others -
Their stakes to recover ?
[Their weeping not making a sound !] "

The Dodgems cry out for side-crashing :
Their Circuit prepared for the bashing !
Pretend it's stock-racing -
Disaster embracing -
Past log-jams eagerly dashing.

" Once a year at the Travelling Fair
Go skyward : strapped to a chair !
Then hook plastic duck ;
With slings try your luck ?
For tilting tea-cups prepare ! "

Don't miss Wiv's Carnival Procession :
Of Route it takes full possession.
Wear Pirates' striped clothing
[Their worst heists still loathing]
Or dress as a Priest for Confession !

The *Pav's* got a huge Deck-Chair :
Get seated thereon - if you dare !
What a great photo opp !
What a fine pageant prop !
Gymnasts only stop and stare !

And what of *Pavilion's* flume :
So fast, you're sent to your doom ?
Round twisting bends
Your body wends:
Custom hitting a boom !

With religion some people grapple :
Helped on at a Wesleyan Chapel.
'Twas pride of Queen Street :
Its lead Spire so neat !
Brought down like a windfall apple.

Its Sister on *Hull Road's* Right-hand -
Azure oval Balcony grand -
Deems Preaching central ....
With prayers penitential ;
Tuesday's " Flavours " best food in the land !

Wiv's largest [Civic] Church
Is locked : leaving brides in the lurch ?
Will it become Apartments ? -
Exhibition compartments ? -
Or falconry's unhindered perch ?

Further t'wards Hull is *St. Matt's -*
Where worshippers sit for a chat.
It stages good Drama -
Artistic panoramas -
Chants Mary's *Magnificat.*

For those who've crossed over to Rome,
Rome has come closer to home !
Cath'lics meet near Bus Garage -
The Pope : don't disparage !
But all your Scriptures comb.

Forget not the PresbyCongs :
Their texts & their cheerful songs.
They meet to the South
Intercessions to mouth...
And each foll'wer for *Unity* longs.

Await just 7-30 days
To join in two *Passion* Plays :
Three Crosses 'neath blue skies -
A Master even Peter denies -
Easter's Story to-excite & amaze.

" Have you noticed how one Store's trolleys
Augment many a front yard's follies ?
Have they been taken ?
For Bath-chairs mistaken ?
Some folk even pinch their Pub's brollies ! "

Whatever - you ask - is much sadder
Than a builder without his steel ladder?
He left it one day -
While cleaning sea spray....
And now it's with owner much badder !

Some gardens are hoisting a flag:
Their loyalties oft-times to brag.
Will the Tricolour flutter ?
" St George ! " you might mutter.
[Don't try an Old Soldier to gag!]

Life can be so horribly cruel -
When cars can't take on more fuel !
Our one Petrol Station
Has odd aberration :
Deliveries needing renewal.

The Library hands out advice
On bins, drains, evictions - lice.
Girls go there for Shelter,
Their Mums with a welter
Of crises to make you blink twice.

Withernsea depends on its *Lettings:*
Flats abundant in such pleasant settings.
Rents perforce kept "low" :
Each void, a struck blow....
[Landlords absent: absent, too, any vetting]

And if it's a *Computer* you need,
Strict user-rules best that you heed !
More pages on screen
For deft surfers keen...
Keep Googling; to Twitter be keyed !

And if it's *your M.P.* you seek out:
Status won't cause you to freak out.
He'll hear all your tales
[Of Council which fails?]
Whilst urging long-sufferers to speak out.

Councillors stand, too, on the street :
Knowing not whom they will meet.
Folk come with their queries
[Not political theories]
Will *new* nerds 'gainst them compete ?

Most passers-by greet you with relish:
Their news to convey - or embellish.
Happ'ly, few take the hump
[View you as mugwump ?]
Shunned Goodwill can feel awful Hellish !

Wiv Bus-drivers always smile;
They smile for mile after mile.
They face tough congestion,
Which harms their digestion.
They'll drop you down next a stile !

Young girls on the Bus are excited :
Their natural good humour ignited.
The sound of their chatter
[Relationships matter !]
Stops only when tired you've alighted.

With *Tablets* they're tot'lly engrossed :
Each new photo aiming to post.
It's called "Social Media" :
[Beyond *Wikipedia*]
Of "Friends" by the dozen to boast.

An hour-long phone-call's arresting;
To privacy's absence attesting!
How cheeky to track
Its course fro-and-back!
Eavesdroppers are rarely protesting!

Wiv's lasses dress just as they please -
Tight jeans with a tear at the knees -
Quite daring tank-tops,
Doc Martens, flip-flops ;
Bronze brassieres twanged for a tease.

Observe boys' clothes *out of School :*
They all look so dapper - so cool !
Their waistcoats so tight ;
Their footwear so light !
Some show-offs, some playing the Fool !

A lad sits with chips in a shelter :
His Girlfriend, next-to, a real belter!
While he does her kiss,
Her fish goes amiss.
[A poor take-away has he dealt her!]

Some fam'lies you'll find are "blended" :
Especially where marriage has ended.
New sisters and brothers -
"Significant Others" -
Where kinship's ties torn go unmended.

Withernsea scholars: *so polite!*
[After breakfast, then at night]
Their behaviour a marker
[Adolescence less darker?]
Good teachers taught them aright !

Withernsea High School was a trial :
"11-plus" failure's denial....
Rurality's best learning ;
Fine teaching turning
Non-starters to Uni, awhile.

To College Wiv's scholars repair :
Learn woodwork, plumbing - or hair ;
Or choose dental nursing
[Their lips tightly pursing ?]
Most pressing : there's Elderly Care !

Wiv does have its local Gazette:
Reporters reporting : you bet !
This Town on a high
Can reach for the Sky !
Good News is half what we get.

We hear, too, of *wickedest* deeds :
Drunkenness, fraud and greed ;
Brash youths simply foolish
[Some Readers quite ghoulish?]
For justice does this organ plead.

A Cottage Hospital once stood at Queen's
[Healed pensioners more than teens]
Valued treatment giving
To those struggling living :
Three Infirm'ries in between.

Still open from eight until eight ??
[Should Injury come not too late?]
We must have recourse -
With no other source
Of help when we're in a bad state.

Our Railway fell to Lord Beeching
[Ignoring our earnest beseeching]
On board was a Guard
Whom closure hit hard :
His train no more villages reaching.

Through Caravans row-upon-row
Could *Withernsea's* tourism grow ?
Some towed to chosen pitch ;
Some owned by campers rich ?
Will developers more spaces bestow ?

Big trailers arrive on low-loaders ;
Their owners in fancy off-roaders ?
They have lots of rooms,
Mod-cons one assumes ?
And the Loo: it leaves no bad odour.

Mobile Homes : they have many names,
On Sites full of fun and games.
They're not really temp'rary :
Their insides exemplary.
Just heed lest one goes up in flames !

All Caravans seek a good *Club :*
Selling whisky & home-made grub.
Then there's Comedy Night,
And a Quiz master bright !
Provided you've kept up your Sub.

Our Static's now let to Miranda :
So plush, with an ample Verandah !
Incredibly spacious....
[Its Site fees : voracious !]
When losing the plot, don't meander !

That Bungalow's all made of wood :
Sawn planks either rotten or good.
Outside : a deck-chair
[A world without Care !]
Loose living as best understood.

"Seathorne " was built in the Eighties :
Retired folk finding new maties !
They live as they choose ;
Play Bridge : win or lose...
And eat sausage pie with some taties !

At *Rimswell : a Tower for clean water*
[Not seen it ? You really oughta !]
A fine circle white -
Its pillars upright :
Preceding the water transporter.

At *Halsham :* a stark Mausoleum -
For vespers, lament & *Te Deum.*
Constables laid resting :
Their standing attesting.
Past Midnight: imagine you see em !

Hilston's Church is very recent:
Stock design, extremely decent.
Re-built for three score :
With sturdy oak door.
[German bombers : how malfeasant!]

At *Waxholme*, they have an old Mill :
Solid and ivy-clad, still.
Would suit Restoration :
A four-bed creation ?
[If builders just had the skill !]

Now for the Holderness *"Queen"* ...
From Spurn Head distant seen !
St. Patrick's has beauty ;
To its village a duty
To welcome the humble & mean.

Patrington's dreaming Spire
Inspires its resident Choir....
An elegant building
Of stonework and gilding :
The Holy Spirit on fire!

Patrington still boasts *a beacon*
[Prim. Chapel served by a Deacon]
Just beyond : a Cricket Ground
[At *their* Mill : a Jump-Course found !]
With Horse-Chestnuts, shall we find Pecan ?

To-day : bored class sent to *Garton*
[Considerably nearer than *Barton* !]
They'll go via *Roos* -
Skirt ditches and sluice -
And buy milk in little square cartons.

Keyingham's Church lost its Spire :
[Its internal structure dire ?]
Yet keeps a stone tower-
Seen past yonder bower -
Maybe that's all bats require ?

At *Mappleton* live many swine :
That folk at High Table might dine.
They share a big shed -
No straw for a bed -
Their numbers may soon see decline.

In *Withernwick*, see many foals :
In a field shared with a few moles.
They look so new-born -
Their hooves not well-worn -
But soon they will jump over Poles.

At *Welwick* they recall the Plot :
Gunpowder that might kill the lot !
Were its schemers disloyal ?
[Fit to dip in hot oil?]
Dig for gravel ; for victory not !

Holmpton's Bunker is famous
[No Cold War allowed to shame us] :
Did Churchill live there ?
Or Hull's ex-Lord Mayor ?
Four minute warning enough to tame us ?

At *Easington* they import raw fuel
[The North Sea : not always cruel]
All its Pipelines are policed :
By ten coppers, at least !
Single Gas tariffs - or dual ?

At *Kilnsea,* a Twitcher's near *Spurn :*
That home of the Redwing & Tern....
A past Army base
Fortified in case
Nazis invade - slash & burn.

Spurn hosts Pilots - also explorers -
Conservationists whose terrain if porous -
Between North Sea & Humber :
Shells, fossils, *without number.*
"Desert Island" alert to Dawn Chorus.

Aldbrough : 20 miles up the Coast....
Camp there - where Sun shines the most !
"Tis a very diff'rent destination :
Stage in longer peregrination ? ....
Where Painter to Subject gets close..

Burstwick's where people make putts :
A Dormitory Village with guts.
It still feels quite rural...
With Clubs in the plural...
Peaceful when everything shuts ?

" Each Wednesday : Hedon Market.
Bob took the car - but couldn't park it !
So he drove on to Swine:
There bought some white wine...
A bell tolled - but he couldn't hark it."

The *Co-op* in *Hedon* is small -
But meets folk's requirements all.
If they travel to *Thorn*,
Their nerves get more worn -
But Cash comes straight out the wall !

Augustine remains Hedon's Saint
[Let nothing his memory taint]
His Church - more an Abbey -
Is known to each Cabbie...
He heals each inner complaint.

For *Hornsea Pott'ry* : a house of its own -
Oh how its Collection has grown !
A wondrous reminder
Of decades much kinder
To designers beforehand unknown.

Hornsea : home of old motor-cars
Which no Council-on-Earth would debar.
Faced with this traffic -
Local traders seraphic ? -
Day-trippers head there from afar.

Hornsea now has brand new *bandstand*
Where gymnasts can practise their
handstand.
It's near those two *lions* -
Two manes folk may try on ? -
Before mounting yon yachting Grandstand !

Hornsea did have a Railway Station :
Joseph Wade's inspired inspiration.
For years left to rot -
Grand archways forgot -
In such a central location.

Burton Constable : Hull's Stately Manor -
Its dynasty blazed on banner -
Boasting movers & shakers,
Skilled cabinet-makers.
Gain entry : all for a Tenner !

Hull's *Maritime* Museum is swish
For those who the Oceans do fish.
A Hist'ry of Navigation :
Sails, ships ...Exploration !
[More Dockyards about to va-nish ?]

The *Ferens* is full of fine Art -
Where ev'ryone's journeys can start.
Sculptures intriguing
[Galleries fatiguing ?]
" *See the Triptych before you depart!* "

One morning spend in "*Street Life* " :
Hull's record of noise and of strife.
See trolleys and trams,
Bath chairs and prams.
Progress spread out with a knife.

Then wander down *Whitefriar Gate:*
Large shops, old pubs, so ornate.
It's an interesting walk
To dockland's last baulk...
A passage to celebrate !

Hull's got a few Bridges swinging :
Dutch trippers their praises singing !
Barges pass underneath -
Not coming to grief -
Wide open more lock-gates be flinging !

Victoria stands in her Square
[Enjoying publicity's glare ?]
Her stamp's universal :
An Empire's dispersal ?
What *King* any better? - declare !

Past *Wincolmlee*, the River narrows :
Men repairing traps and harrows.
It's a quaint little maze :
Well worth searcher's gaze !
And allotments grow all folk's marrows !

House of Fraser condemned to close :
As *Hammond's* , the place shoppers chose.
These big, varied, stores
Led to dropping of jaws !
Trade now to *St. Stephen's* oft goes.

Some liked the old *C. & A.:*
Tasteful fashion - with little to pay.
Sports Direct is now trading
Posh jeans, tops with braiding.
[Watch workers determined to play !]

Hull's *Guildhall* is very plush !
[Its splendour makes visitors blush]
Solid oak chairs
For Worshipful Mayors....
" Council's in Session : Hush ! "

Males turn, for relief, underground:
With only a tinkle as sound.
What feet trod before !
[What baggage they bore !]
Theatre's flush in-the-round.

City Hall 's tuneful Musicians
Depend on good Sound Technicians.
Each fine Concert work
Comes as a perk
To each wealthy Artist Patrician.

The *Hall* also hosts Graduation :
[Degrees met with much adulation]
And upmarket Weddings
[Singlehood shedding]
And Trade Fairs beyond estimation.

The *Truck* continues its showing
Of Shows whose Ratings are glowing :
Many experimental ;
Others experiential.
Credit on Playwrights bestowing.

Year of Culture 's colour was blue
[Not dark - but a lighter hue]
Those Volunt'ry Hosts -
At each feast the Ghosts?-
Never said they hadn't a clue !

Hull Minster 's been much swopped round :
Religion part-filling the ground.
Therein many shows...
God saying : " how goes ? "
To priests who these precincts do pound.

In *Minster* : beyond the Nave
Are Mem'ries this City must save :
The loss of the *Gaul* -
Its Crew one and all -
Were ever there seamen so brave ?

In shipbuilding's driest dock :
Please turn not to study the clock.
Performers here stage
Works straight from the page....
Any late-comers : "Knock ! knock!"

On one renowned landing-stage
Came ferries of *former* age :
From *New Holland* sailing -
Their engines not failing -
Lincolnshire's businessmen sage.

Each night at Marfleet's staithe
You'll come more Seamen to wave
Out on their sailing
To Bruges - with mailings -
P&O's Liner suave.

Old Inn on the front : *The Minerva*
[Each rustic lass so proud to serve yer!]
Has keg beers eleven :
CAMRA's seventh Heaven !
[" Big Order : please don't unnerve her ! "]

Tramps thought one morn dawned *brighter* -
Their burdens growing lighter -
So they went to Hull's *jail :*
Its walls did they scale -
And now they'll be sleeping much tighter !

To Hull remanded till Trial
Are convicts convinced of denial.
The Judge in his ermine
Does not speak of "vermin" :
That being *The Sun's* usual style.

Each day Students travel to work :
Zero-hours - where they're driven berserk !
Some live in the Sticks -
Like hens with five chicks ! -
Grudged tips their solitary perk.

More Students go on *to the Venn* -
In *Willoughby*   taught now & then.
Brynmoor Jones holds their books,
In *Middleton* : good cooks !
And the *Union* shop sells ev'ry pen !

MethSoc is just one Society
Students join of infinite variety.
Trinity hosts a Squash -
Dress not too posh ! -
At least they'll be taught sobriety !

On Graduates does Hull much depend ?
[On their Campus each year to descend]
They help our Economy -
Displaying autonomy -
You'll meet them round every bend !

Its forty statues *give* Hull a boost :
Monuments where pigeons roost !
All types of Memorial :
Each an instant Tutorial.
How Sculptors sculpt when loosed!

And now to avoid confusion :
This Book must reach *a Conclusion.*
Wiv *has* Sense of Place,
Good living - and space !
So Poetry's not an Intrusion !

Yet keep on writing Verse
[Rhyme-patterns sometimes a curse !]
Wiv's full of material :
[Hard-edged - or ethereal]
Imagining seeks not its purse.

And while we're discussing an Ending
[Wiv's feeble critics transcending...]
We'll find *Place of Sense*
With virtues immense...
Its High Tide, no need of defending.

So now at close of the Eve :
You *too* must cheer - *and believe !*
.....Wiv increasingly boasting
Achievements worth toasting....
Erstwhile happenings retrieve.

****

APPENDIX :

AN ALTERNATIVE ENDING ?

WHAT WOULD HAPPEN IF *SOME* READERS -

MAYBE ONLY A FEW ? -

HELD A VISION

OF NO WITHERNSEA :

A GHOST-TOWN WITHERNSEA....

DYSTOPIA ?

---

read on :

An enormous Tidal Wave -
As mighty as is grave -
Sweeps o'er our streets :
Great panic ; retreats !
[No medals for the brave]

The Ocean comes at speed :
No barriers will it heed.
Withernsea trapped , surely drowned ,
Encompassed by creepy sound !
Exactly as Nature decreed ?

Dads lack the borrowed time
To escape the awful slime.
They gasp in despair ;
[Rooves be-yond repair!]
Entombed in grimmest grime.

Babes lie sick in their cots ;
Mums still washing the pots ;
Girls confused in their gardens
Heedless of Fate - which hardens !
[Pets wholly helpless : lots]

Car engines will not start ;
No buses are staffed to depart.
Cycles stand gaunt in their sheds
[Cyclists down alleyways fled ?]
No borrowing of farmer's cart !

Two taxis are still stuck in Hull :
With gas contractors full....
They unsuspecting -
Wiv needs protecting.
[Lift only for herring gull !]

News : five sons sit on roof !
Lost neighbours [hiding ?] aloof :
They thanking a hatch
With ease-giving latch.
Survival : the ultimate proof.

Two dozen or so reach the park
Their prospects yet terribly stark :
Trapped in swilling swell
[Storms nothing can quell]
Sky above them : forbiddingly dark !

And then come streaks of lightning ;
Thunder following : so loud & so fright'ning.
Not seen, heard, before : .
[Folk shook to the core]
Nor sign of Noon's twilight bright'ning.

A few- very few - run to Roos
Like horses freed : on the loose !
There exiles feel safe :
Mayor placed next to waif !
[Still dreading the Ocean's whoosh]

Some Teens reach Water Tower -
Coats shed : to give them more power.
They dare not look back
The foe on their track ?
'Neath many trees'-growth to cower.

In Boatyard's recent arrival :
Chance air-pocket's aiding survival :
Helmsmen locked below deck
Of craft - now a wreck ? -
Recall Wiv's fishing revival.

And what of those missing landlords
Whom no one - drifting - applauds ?
Who ploughed ill-got money
Then reaped Milk-&-Honey :
Now forfeit their ill-got rewards.

The Church was already boarded :
St. Nicholas no longer lauded ?
A Resort freed from God ?
Giving Mammon the nod ?
Satan due honour accorded.

Upstream : a Swimming Pool drained....
Swimmers stark naked & pained ;
No lifting great weights ;
No chatting up Dates.
[Fitness schedules: *torn-up-* or stained]

Meridian's doors stay shut :
Their film-shows abruptly cut.
No need for Town Meetings -
No Guests needing seating -
No grievance vented: "Tut-tut!"

The Comp now lacks Scholars :
No miscreants to collar!
No Classes to teach -
Nor Targets to reach:
Guide-books that nobody foll-ers.

Most caravans tilt, rudely shattered :
Rent income all that mattered ?
Their power-supply suspended....
Their holiday plans upended....
Loosened doorways battered.

And SHORES which graced Wiv's Prom
Now offers no hand -nor aplomb.
Where folk brought their worries ;
Broke bread; sampled curries !
[That wave: more destructive than Bomb]

Fountains once dearly sunk -
In setts, for kids [no drunks !]
Will never rise a-gain
Nor grown-ups entertain...
Another piece of junk.

TESCO fastens tight its doors
[Rivals jeer - but no guffaws]
Its vast Stock will perish.
Past purchases cherish !
Was ever a longer P-A-U-S-E ?

See Boots remain metal-shuttered :
Hopes of cures, unneeded, not uttered.
Queen Street with no traffic!
[Nor snarl-ups: once graphic!]
Wiv, croaking, scarcely spluttered.

ALDI holds one "Last Day" SALE -
Footfall falling: bound to fail -
And only ONE Assistant
[Her "Offers" persistent !]
From Goole, she missing gale.

County Council still exists :
In Beverley's circling mists !
Never loving our Coast ?
Of Wiv ne'er to boast ? ....
Rejection that persists.

All Streets are very eerie ;
No Public House how beery.
A Resort so hollow :
No Tourists will follow !
No laughter intense - or cheery.

The Fields, as well, are bare
[No creatures grazing there]
No farmyard bustle ;
No Auctions, no hustle ;
No wheat - but only tares.

Wiv sleeps now all through the year :
No signals of help to appear !
The Trains : they went first :
Sea's comeback much worse ?
That only leaves Place braced to Fear.

When an Ocean knows not its bounds -
When it logic and mercy confounds -
When a Town so diligently built
Is left to sadden and wilt :
We see raw Nature's power :
No bulb, no stem, no flower.

****

PRINTED & BOUND BY WARD & PINKNEY [PRINTERS]
WEST 1, NORTHUMBERLAND AVENUE,
KINGSTON-UPON-HULL HU2 OLN
TEL: 01482 -325014